WHEN THE WOLVES SANG

by Bill Mason

An OWL Book
Published by Greey de Pencier Books, 1980
©Bill Mason
ISBN 0-919872-51-4
Printed in Canada

As the wolves moved along the wind-swept ridge, the crisp snow crunched beneath their feet. They were travelling at an easy lope, strung out single file behind their two leaders. Suddenly, on the brow of the hill, the male leader stopped, his breath hanging on the morning air and his steely coat glinting in the rising sun. His mate moved up beside him and also stopped. They both saw a herd of caribou resting in the middle of the lake ahead.

Sensing the excitement of the hunt, the pack clustered together. The two leaders raised their tails. The others kept their tails low and laid their ears back against their heads. They licked the corners of the leaders' mouths, and the leaders occasionally snarled and pinned them to the ground. The dark-coated female leader grabbed a frisky young wolf by the snout. She held him in her jaws for a moment, then released him.

Two older members of the pack watched hungrily from the edge of the trees. They were anxious to begin the hunt but dared not run ahead of the leaders. At last the wolves came down onto the ice and crossed the lake, angling away from the caribou. But the caribou were not fooled. They knew they were being hunted, but they waited and watched, saving their strength for the tremendous burst of speed they'd need to escape those powerful jaws.

The pack was about halfway from shore when suddenly the male leader stopped and looked toward the distant horizon. He could faintly hear a whining sound that did not belong in the forest. Now the rest of the pack heard it too, but because the leaders showed only a mild interest,

they were not afraid. And they all stood gazing at the sky as a large bird flew into sight. It was only when the bird came toward the pack that the wolves became nervous. Their tails dropped and their ears moved back against their heads. The

leaders started to run for the trees at the edge of the lake and the pack followed. But then, the noisy creature swung in a wide circle between the wolves and the safety of the shore. The wolves huddled uneasily around the leaders, wondering what to do next. Then the bird turned away, swooped down and landed on the lake among the caribou. As it came to rest, the noise stopped and silence returned to the land.

From the side of the great bird stepped another strange creature. The wolves had never seen anything like this before. It walked on only two legs and it stood there alone

as the bird began to roar louder than ever. Again the pack broke into a run. As the bird lifted into the sky, the sound died away and the wolves turned to stare at the intruder.

It was *me* there on the ice, and as I blinked against the glare of the sun, I could hardly believe what I was seeing. After weeks of searching, here I was among wolves who had never seen a human being before. I quickly grabbed my camera with its long telephoto lens and focused on what looked like the leader, a huge grey wolf with a magnificent bushy tail.

As I watched him, I shivered. But I knew I was safe because, for some mysterious reason, wolves always avoid man.

After looking me over, the big wolf turned and loped away. Everything was going perfectly—perhaps now, I thought, I would see the wolves go after the caribou. But instead, three climbed onto a small rocky island and, after nuzzling each other, curled up and went to sleep. Then the rest of the pack lay down. I wouldn't see them hunt yet.

If I were to get my igloo built by nightfall, I decided, I'd better get started. The hard-packed snow was ideal, and the work went quickly. As I cut the blocks and spiralled the walls upward. I thought of my wife, Joyce, and my children Paul and Becky. They could not be with me here among the wild wolves, but back home, they were among wolves too...

My family was lucky, I guess. Because I am a wildlife photographer interested in helping people understand about wolves, I keep some in a huge fenced area behind our house. These wolves, loaned to me by the Department of Forestry, were born in captivity but only two were tame. The first of these was a timid little wolf we called Sparky. She loved to try to steal Joyce's hat and pulled at Becky's hair any chance she got.

The other tame wolf was huge and handsome and called Big Charlie. I could play with Charlie because he was quite used to being handled. But the female who was his mate was not at all tame. She was afraid of people and would back silently away if anyone came close to her. She and Charlie were the leaders of the pack, and as leaders they bossed the other wolves as they would have in the wild.

One of our greatest thrills was the day we saw Charlie's mate digging a den—a sure sign she was going to have puppies. Fortunately for us, she chose a place in the side of a hill

where we could see right inside. As each baby was born, she carefully bit off the umbilical cord and licked its coat until it shone. She would place them between her forepaws, then get ready for the next to be born. It wasn't long before there were six wiggling puppies all thirstily nursing in a row beside their mother.

One day when the pups were about three weeks old, I was

watching the den when a little ball of fur wobbled out. It was soon followed by another and then another until all six pups sat blinking in the sunlight. Moments later when she spied me, the  mother gently picked them up one by one in her jaws and carried them away. This is exactly what a mother wolf would do in the wild to protect her pups from bears or eagles.

 Big Charlie took a great interest in his pups and played with them constantly, always being careful not to step on them. The pups knew by licking and pulling at the corners of the adults' mouths that they would bring up food from their stomachs.

In the wild, wolves some-
times have to hunt far away
from home, and this is the
best way to bring food to
their young.

To make it easier for me to
photograph the pups, Becky
and Paul bottle fed and
cared for two of them. They
called them Loupy and Fang. We could tell right away that
Fang would someday be a leader. When Loupy approached,
Fang would raise his little tail as straight as he could. He

would then try to grab
Loupy by the throat with
his sharp teeth. He was not
being mean, but, like all
wolf leaders, he was showing that he was in command
—and wolf packs need
leaders to survive.

We enjoyed filming and studying our wolves, but to really
understand wolves I knew that I must live among wild ones...

I had been working on my snow house and daydreaming about home for several hours when all of a sudden I looked up. The wolves on the rocky island were getting to their feet and much to my surprise, instead of moving toward the other wolves, they started coming toward me. I quickly reminded myself that wolves aren't supposed to attack people—and hoped these wolves knew that too!

At a distance that was just a little too close for my comfort, the wolves stopped. Then, with one last glance, at me, they turned toward the caribou. I realized that the wolves had only been working their way into position for the chase and I had been in the way. The caribou watched as the wolves approached. They stood motionless but I knew they were ready.

Suddenly the big wolf charged towards the middle of the herd! Immediately the lake was alive with hundreds of running caribou. They moved in a great wave, fanning out and away from the charging wolves. The wolves had almost caught up and were watching the herd for stragglers or a caribou that was  limping. But there was none. The chase was over, and the caribou had escaped.

And then I heard a long, mournful howl. As more wolves joined in, the song grew and grew and then gradually died away. The wolves regrouped, greeted each other, then trotted off single file into the trees. They were on the move again. They knew sooner or later they would find a caribou they could catch. It was just a matter of time.

In the days that followed I would see the wolves and hear them howling many times as I wandered from lake to lake. Then one day I came across the leaders eating a dead caribou. As I peered through the trees, I saw a young wolf

break away from the rest of the pack and grab a piece of meat. The female chased him and made him drop it. She was not being greedy but, again, she was showing she was leader. He would eat later.

After the wolves had left, I snowshoed over to the dead caribou and looked down at what was left of this once beautiful and graceful animal. I felt sad, but I reminded myself that the wolves had only done what they had to do. They had to kill to eat.

As I stood there, a howl came from far away, and then another and another. It was the most beautiful song I had ever heard.

I returned to my igloo, prepared supper in the warm glow of candlelight and thought about the wolves' song. I knew it belonged to the wild in a way that I never could. But I was grateful to be there. I would have memories of those beautiful wolves and this wild country forever.

Canadian Cataloguing in Publication Data

Mason, Bill, 1929-
  When the wolves sang

(Owl's true-life adventure series)

ISBN 0-919872-51-4 bd.

1. Wolves—Juvenile literature. I. Title.
II. Series.

QL795.W8M37   j599.74'442   C80-094582-4

Photos by Bill Mason, except cover and p. 31 by
Scott Stewart, p. 27 by George Calef and p. 29 by
Charlie Ott: Photo Researchers, Inc.